$28.65

WORLD RELIGIONS
CHRISTIANITY

BY DON NARDO

Content Adviser:
Holly Taylor Coolman, Ph.D.,
Department of Theology, Providence College

Reading Adviser:
Alexa L. Sandmann, Ed.D., Professor of Literacy,
College and Graduate School of Education,
Health, and Human Services, Kent State University

Compass Point Books
151 Good Counsel Drive
P.O. Box 669
Mankato, MN 56002-0669

This book was manufactured with paper containing
at least 10 percent post-consumer waste.

Photographs ©: BigStockPhoto: megumi 36–37; The Bridgeman Art Library:
Giraudon/Musee de Picardie, Amiens, France 20, Giraudon/Sant'Apollinare
Nuovo, Ravenna, Italy 12; Getty Images: AFP/Arturo Mari 5, AFP/Guido
Bergmann 40, AFP/Luis Liwanag cover, AFP/Patrick Hertzog 4–5, The
Bridgeman Art Library 43, Franco Origlia 6, Hulton Archive 26–27, Tim
Boyle 39; iStockphoto: Daniel R. Burch 18, Darren Hendley 30, Duncan Walker
33, Hulton Archive 13, Yusuf Anil Akduygu 10–11; Library of Congress 34;
North Wind Picture Archives 15, 16–17, 29; Photolibrary: Jim Pickerell 24;
Shutterstock: gary718 38, Jozef Sedmak 23, maga (background texture) 4, 10, 16,
26, 36, 46, 47, maxstockphoto (cross pattern) cover (top and bottom), back cover
(top), 1, 45, sidebars throughout, Steven Kratochwill (ornate window pattern),
cover (middle and bottom left), back cover (left) and throughout.

Editor: Brenda Haugen
Designers: Ashlee Suker and Bobbie Nuytten
Media Researcher: Svetlana Zhurkin
Library Consultant: Kathleen Baxter
Art Director: LuAnn Ascheman-Adams
Creative Director: Joe Ewest
Editorial Director: Nick Healy
Managing Editor: Catherine Neitge
Cartographer: XNR Productions, Inc.

Library of Congress Cataloging-in-Publication Data
Nardo, Don, 1947–
   Christianity / by Don Nardo.
      p. cm.—(World religions)
   Includes index.
   ISBN 978-0-7565-4237-5 (library binding)
   1. Christianity—Juvenile literature. I. Title. II. Series.
   BR125.5.N37 2010
   230—dc22   2009015811

Visit Compass Point Books on the Internet at *www.compasspointbooks.com*
or e-mail your request to *custserv@compasspointbooks.com*

Table of Contents

On April 2, 2005, one of the largest gatherings of Christians in modern history took place in Rome, Italy. About 2 million people waited in St. Peter's Square. Rising above them beside the square was the towering dome of St. Peter's Basilica.

Chapter One

A NEW SPIRITUAL LEADER

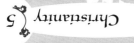

Pope John Paul II was born Karol Josef Wojtyla in 1920 and was the first Polish pope.

Both are part of the Vatican, the center of the Roman Catholic Church and the headquarters for its spiritual leader, the pope. Catholics and other Christians believe that the basilica was built atop the burial site of St. Peter. He was one of the closest followers of Jesus Christ, who is the center of the Christian faith. So St. Peter's Basilica is one of Christianity's holiest sites. The people crowding the square had come to pay their respects to Pope John Paul II, who had just died.

Choosing a New Pope

When a pope dies, a meeting called a papal conclave takes place. It's attended by members of the College of Cardinals. The cardinals are senior Catholic clergy who advise the pope. They also elect a new pope when one dies. The papal conclave that met after John Paul's death consisted of 115 cardinals. The meeting began 10 days after the pope was buried. The cardinals voted, each writing down the name of the cardinal he wanted to become the new pope. After the votes were counted, the oldest cardinal in the conclave went to the balcony of the basilica. He told the waiting spectators "Habemus Papam!" A Latin phrase, it means "We have a pope!"

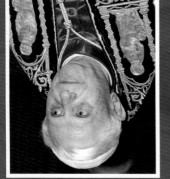

Joseph Alois Ratzinger of Germany became the new pope and took the name Benedict XVI.

Some mourners carried flowers. Some prayed silently. Some cried openly. John Paul had been one of the most popular of the modern popes. During his papal reign (1978–2005), he had visited more than 100 countries. Time after time, his personal warmth and charm had won the hearts of the people—regardless of whether they were Catholic.

Many of those who had liked John Paul in life came to pay their respects after his death. More than 4 million

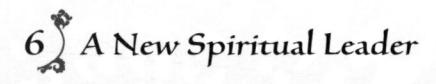

Knowing Pope John Paul II was near death, people gathered in St. Peter's Square awaiting news.

people filed past the casket in which his body lay. Dressed in his bright red papal robe, John Paul lay in state in St. Peter's for four days. Among those who came were 70 presidents and prime ministers, four kings, and five queens. It was the largest gathering of heads of state in history. John Paul's funeral was also the biggest gathering of worshippers in the history of the Christian faith.

Many of the Christians who attended the funeral were Catholics. This was not surprising. After all, as pope, John Paul was the leader of the Catholic Church. However, many representatives of other Christian denominations also paid their respects. Among them was the archbishop of Canterbury. The archbishop is the head of the Anglican Church, also called the Church of England, which broke away from the Catholic Church in the 1500s. After that Catholics and Anglicans were rival Christian groups. Yet John Paul chose to celebrate their similarities rather than emphasize their differences. He called the Anglican Church "our sister church." He preached at Canterbury Cathedral when he visited England. After John Paul's death, a memorial service for the pope was held in the cathedral. Similar services were held in other Christian churches across the world.

These churches represent many kinds of Christians.

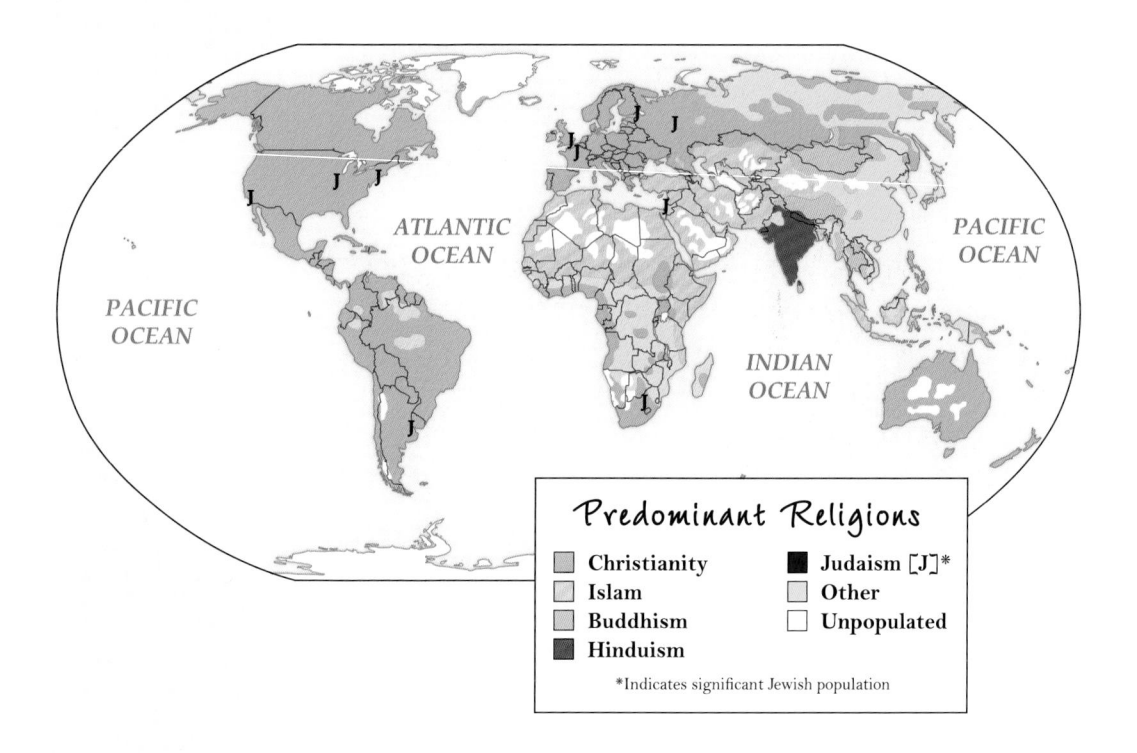

Predominant Religions

- Christianity
- Islam
- Buddhism
- Hinduism
- Judaism [J]*
- Other
- Unpopulated

*Indicates significant Jewish population

Though Catholicism is the largest Christian group, there are thousands of other denominations. Among them are Methodists, Baptists, Lutherans, Episcopalians, Amish, Eastern Orthodox, and Mormons. As separate religious groups, they have differences. Some observe religious holidays on different dates. They have different rituals and practices during their weekly or daily services. Yet all Christian groups are united by some basic beliefs and customs. They all worship the same God, for instance. They all recognize Jesus

Today's Christians

Of the more than 2 billion Christians in the world today, about 1.1 billion are Roman Catholics. They recognize the pope as their leader. The second largest branch of modern Christianity is Protestantism, with about 700 million members. There are thousands of Protestant denominations. Some familiar ones in the United States are Presbyterians, Methodists, Baptists, Congregationalists, and Quakers. The third-largest branch of Christianity is the Eastern Orthodox Church, with about 260 million members. Among its many denominations are Greek Orthodox, Russian Orthodox, Polish Orthodox, and Serbian Orthodox.

Christ as God's son. One of John Paul's most memorable achievements was to emphasize these shared beliefs. That, he felt, would make all Christians stronger.

 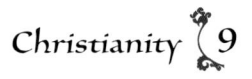

Chapter Two

CHRISTIANITY'S FOUNDERS

Each Christian denomination has some unique beliefs and ceremonies. But all Christians have the same core beliefs, which center on the teachings of Jesus Christ.

A young Jew from the town of Nazareth, Jesus began preaching in Palestine sometime in the 20s C.E.

To acknowledge all world religions, Compass Point Books uses new abbreviations to distinguish time periods. For ancient times, instead of B.C., we use B.C.E., which means before the common era. B.C. means before Christ. Similarly we use C.E., which means in the common era, instead of A.D. The abbreviation A.D. stands for the Latin phrase anno Domini, which means in the year of our Lord, referring to Jesus Christ. Of course not all peoples worship Jesus.

He attracted a small but loyal group of followers, including the 12 apostles, who are also called the disciples. Jesus said the kingdom of God would arrive soon. Word spread that he was performing miracles. Jesus, it was said, had walked on water and made sick people well.

Partly for these reasons, several of Jesus' followers suspected that he was the Messiah, a superhuman or semidivine person who they thought would someday arrive to help bring about the kingdom of God, an era of peace and justice on Earth.

In the first century, Rome controlled all the lands surrounding the Mediterranean Sea. These lands were inhabited by people

A mosaic of Jesus Christ dating to 1261 can be seen in the Hagia Sophia, a museum in Istanbul, Turkey.

Christians believe Jesus performed many miracles, including giving sight to the blind.

with diverse cultural and religious traditions and ideas.

Among these people were the Jews, who lived in Palestine, the region bordering the eastern Mediterranean. They were unique at the time because they did not worship multiple gods, as other people did. The Jews were monotheists, worshipping a single, all-powerful god.

The Jews longed for the day when they could be free from Rome, rule themselves, and be a part of the kingdom of God.

While some Jews believed Jesus was the Messiah, others disagreed. They assumed he was a fake. Some

Jewish leaders began to see Jesus as a troublemaker who threatened their authority. In about 30 C.E., a group of armed men arrested him and turned him over to Roman authorities. Roman guards nailed him to a wooden cross and left him to die. At the time, this form of execution, known as crucifixion, was common.

According to later Christian writings and beliefs, Jesus was able to overcome death. He rose from his tomb. Later he visited several of his followers and urged them to go out and preach in his name.

Jesus' followers were now certain that he was the Messiah. They began telling this to others. Calling themselves the People of the Way, they at first preached only to Jews. They had no desire to start a new religion.

Jesus was crucified between two thieves.

They wanted to prepare Jews for the kingdom of God, which they were sure would be coming soon.

However, most Jews doubted and rejected the claims of the People of the Way. Authorities in Jerusalem beat two of the group's leaders, Peter and John, and ordered them to stop preaching. The group opened chapters in other cities. Still they found it difficult to convert Jews to their beliefs.

In about 36 C.E., a man named Saul of Tarsus, later called Paul, joined the People of the Way. He had long dismissed the group's claims about Jesus' divinity. Yet one day as he was walking toward Damascus, a city in Syria, he had a miraculous vision. Paul said Jesus appeared to

Roads Help Spread the Faith

The early Christians took advantage of the large system of excellent roads that had been built by the Romans. To expand the new faith, members had to seek converts in distant towns and cities. Roman roads were a ready means of travel. These highways were paved and in most areas were well guarded. They also had rest stops and inns along the way. So those who used the roads could travel in safety and comfort.

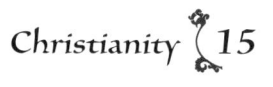

Paul preached Christianity at Antioch, in northern Syria.

him and called on him to join the movement.

Paul did more than preach that Jesus was the son of God. He also saw the need to spread this message beyond Jews. Thanks to Paul, the People of the Way began recruiting gentiles (non-Jews). Some of them converted. Sometime in the 50s C.E., the group's gentile members started calling themselves Christians. In the years that followed, increasing numbers of them no longer felt a connection with Judaism. In this way, Paul set in motion the rise of a major new faith—Christianity.

Chapter Three

SACRED TEXTS AND BELIEFS

Almost all Christians revere certain scriptures, sacred texts that were written many centuries ago. These writings were collected into a larger work known as the Bible. That name comes from the Latin word *biblia*, meaning book.

In 1454 the Bible became the first book ever printed. Since that time it has been translated into more than 2,000 languages.

The Christian Bible consists of two main sections called testaments. The first is the Old Testament. It contains the books of the Jewish scriptures. These were written by Jewish writers between about 1100 and 100 B.C.E., long before Jesus' time. They tell the story of God's creation of Earth and humanity, the early struggles of the Jews, and the rise and fall of the ancient Jewish kingdoms of Israel and Judah.

The books of the New Testament deal mainly with the lives of Jesus and his apostles and their teachings. These books were written by various Christian writers in the late first century C.E. and in the century that followed. The core of the New Testament was set by about the year 200. It includes the books of Matthew, Mark, Luke, and John, usually called the Gospels. It also includes the book of Acts and several letters by Paul and other early Christian leaders. Church authorities added a few

A Bible printed in the 1450s was likely the first use of movable type, invented by Johannes Gutenberg.

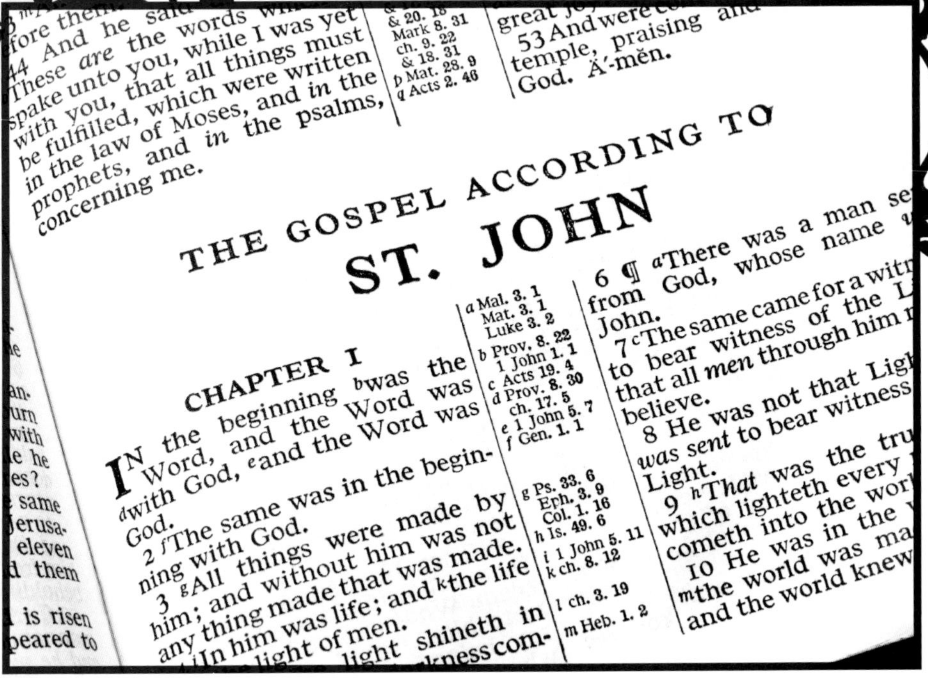

The following text appears within the Bible image:

fore the...
44 And he said...
These *are* the words wh...
spake unto you, while I was yet
with you, that all things must
be fulfilled, which were written
in the law of Moses, and in the
prophets, and in the psalms,
concerning me.

& 20. 18
Mark 8. 31
ch. 9. 22
& 18. 31
p Mat. 28. 9
q Acts 2. 46

great jo...
53 And were c...
temple, praising and
God. A'-mĕn.

THE GOSPEL ACCORDING TO
ST. JOHN

CHAPTER I

IN the beginning *b*was the
Word, and the Word was
*d*with God, *e*and the Word was
God.
2 *f*The same was in the beginning with God.
3 *g*All things were made by
him; and without him was not
any thing made that was made.
*k*the life
*i*In him was life; and *k*the life
...light of men.
...light shineth in
...kness com-

a Mal. 3. 1
Mat. 3. 1
Luke 3. 2
b Prov. 8. 22
1 John 1. 1
c Acts 19. 4
d Prov. 8. 30
ch. 17. 5
e 1 John 5. 7
f Gen. 1. 1

g Ps. 33. 6
Eph. 3. 9
Col. 1. 16
h Is. 49. 6
i 1 John 5. 11
k ch. 8. 12

l ch. 3. 19
m Heb. 1. 2

6 ¶ *a*There was a man se...
from God, whose name...
John.
7 *c*The same came for a witn...
to bear witness of the L...
that all *men* through him...
believe.
8 He was not that Light,
was sent to bear witness...
Light.
9 *h*That was the tru...
which lighteth every...
cometh into the worl...
10 He was in the...
*m*the world was ma...
and the world knew...

The Bible, open to the book of John, who was one of Jesus' apostles

other texts later. The New Testament was complete by about 400.

Most Christian groups also share some core beliefs and customs. Most of these ideas have remained unchanged, or nearly so, since the faith's emergence. Some, such as the existence of a single God, came from Judaism. Others came from New Testament texts or the writings of early Christian leaders.

Several of these basic beliefs appeared in a statement that appeared around 150. It came to be known as the Apostles' Creed. "I believe in God, the Father Almighty,

Christian Symbols

The best known of the many traditional Christian symbols:

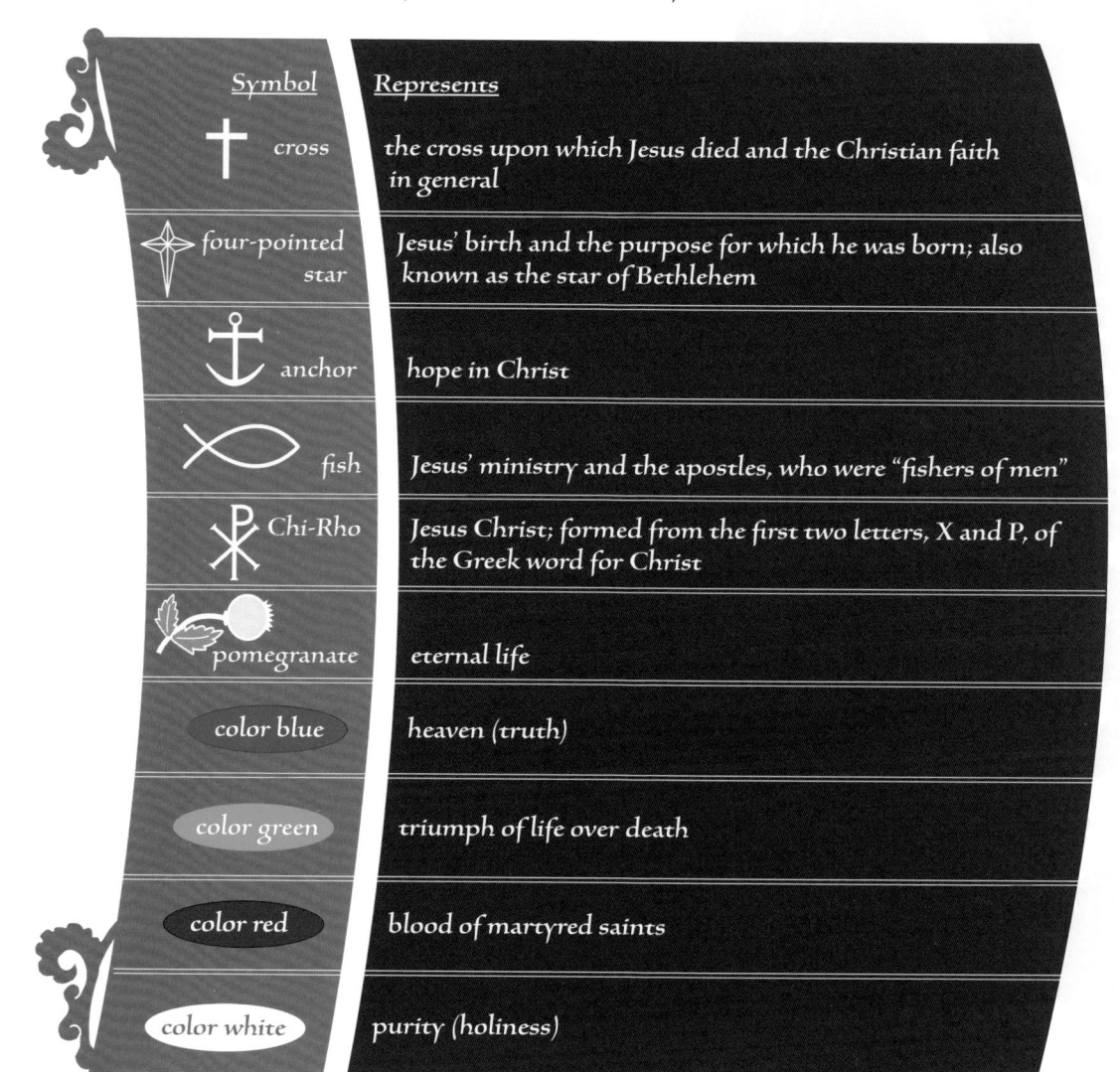

Symbol	Represents
cross	the cross upon which Jesus died and the Christian faith in general
four-pointed star	Jesus' birth and the purpose for which he was born; also known as the star of Bethlehem
anchor	hope in Christ
fish	Jesus' ministry and the apostles, who were "fishers of men"
Chi-Rho	Jesus Christ; formed from the first two letters, X and P, of the Greek word for Christ
pomegranate	eternal life
color blue	heaven (truth)
color green	triumph of life over death
color red	blood of martyred saints
color white	purity (holiness)

maker of heaven and earth," it begins. The creed goes on to express belief in "Jesus Christ, his only Son, our Lord. He was conceived by the Holy Spirit, born of the Virgin Mary, suffered under Pontius Pilate, was crucified, died, and was buried. He descended into hell; the third day he rose again from the dead; he ascended into heaven."

Thus all Christians accept that Jesus was God's son. However, the vast majority of Christians also believe in the Holy Trinity. The Trinity is the Father, Son, and Holy Spirit. But these are not seen as separate divine beings. Instead they are differing aspects of God's character. Christian leaders often say this means "one God, three persons."

Another core belief shared by most Christians concerns Jesus' mission on Earth. It holds that he took human form and died on a cross to help humans achieve salvation—the cleansing of sins and going to heaven to live with God.

The Trinity is depicted in a 15th century painting. The Trinity includes the Father (large image), Son (Jesus on the cross), and Holy Spirit (dove).

The Seven Sacraments

Catholics, Orthodox Christians, Anglicans, and some other Christian groups recognize seven sacraments, sacred rites or rituals:

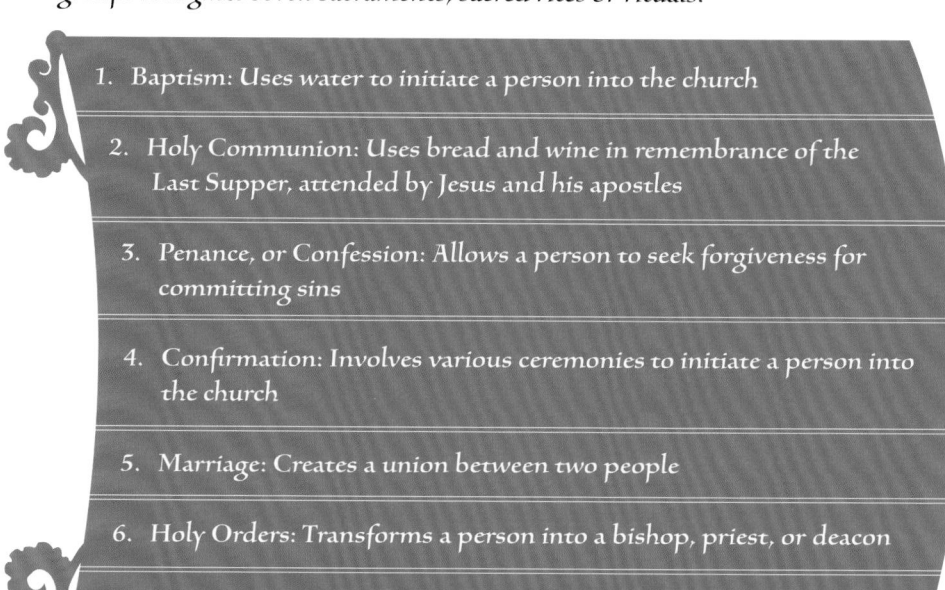

1. Baptism: Uses water to initiate a person into the church

2. Holy Communion: Uses bread and wine in remembrance of the Last Supper, attended by Jesus and his apostles

3. Penance, or Confession: Allows a person to seek forgiveness for committing sins

4. Confirmation: Involves various ceremonies to initiate a person into the church

5. Marriage: Creates a union between two people

6. Holy Orders: Transforms a person into a bishop, priest, or deacon

7. Anointing the Sick: Consists of a priest's blessing someone who is gravely ill

Thus, according to Christian teachings, Jesus died for humanity's sins.

Most Christians also share the custom of baptism. It often includes sprinkling a person with water, but in some denominations, the person is immersed in water. In a symbolic sense, the water is thought to cleanse the person's soul. For that reason, baptism is used to introduce a person into the church.

Priests and Ministers

One major difference among Christian groups is the nature of their religious officials. Catholics and Anglicans have bishops and priests. In performing their duties, they act in Jesus Christ's name. In Protestantism all believers are viewed as priests. Some are specifically educated to "minister to" (help and guide) others. They are called ministers or pastors.

But there are differences in beliefs among Christians. Not all Christians agree on how people can attain salvation. Catholics, Anglicans, Orthodox Christians, and some Lutherans believe that the church can help by acting as a channel of communication between God and humans. One way is through the ritual of baptism, which is thought to wash away one's sins. Some Protestants have a different view. They hold that salvation comes directly from God—that he forgives those who believe in him. This concept is called *sola fide*, meaning "by faith alone."

There are other differences between Catholic beliefs and other Christian beliefs. For example, Catholics see the pope as the main religious authority. Many Protestants believe that such authority lies in scripture—all that a Christian needs to know to lead a good life and be saved lies in the Bible.

Christian groups also differ on the meaning of the ritual of Holy Communion. Also called the Eucharist, it recreates part of Jesus' final meal with his apostles before he was crucified. Worshippers swallow a sip of wine or, in some cases, grape juice. This represents Jesus' blood. They also eat a small piece of bread or a wafer, which represents Jesus' body. Catholics believe that during the ceremony the wine and bread actually change into Jesus' blood and flesh. Most Protestants disagree. They believe that Holy Communion fondly remembers the Last Supper. They believe that Jesus' spirit is present during the ritual, but the bread and wine remain only bread and wine.

Jesus celebrated his last meal with his apostles before one of them, Judas Iscariot, betrayed him to Roman soldiers.

 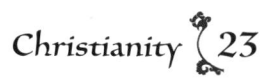

There is much more agreement among various groups of Christians about the faith's major holiday celebrations. The most sacred for all Christians is Easter. This spring festival celebrates Christians'

People at a Bethesda, Maryland, church celebrated Easter Sunday with a balloon launch.

belief in Jesus' resurrection three days after his death on the cross. The date for Easter varies from year to year and from church to church. Western Christian denominations, including Protestants and Catholics, celebrate Easter on the first Sunday following the first full moon that occurs after March 21. Eastern Christian groups, such as Greek Orthodox, use a slightly different calendar to calculate the date for Easter. So Easter rarely falls on the same date in both the West and East.

However, nearly all Christians worldwide take part in the same basic rituals on Easter. They hold festive church services and have special feasts. Many denominations have Holy Communion, and some, especially in the East, stage solemn public parades, called processions.

Next to Easter, the most important and most widely celebrated Christian holiday is Christmas. It celebrates Jesus' birth. Nearly all Christians observe Christmas on December 25. However, this is a traditional religious holiday date borrowed from the ancient Romans. Scholars don't know the exact day and year when Jesus was born.

Some of the rituals held to celebrate Christmas are the same as those for Easter. Church services, Holy Communion, and feasting are among them. Other standard Christmas customs include singing Christmas carols and exchanging gifts with loved ones and friends.

By about 90 C.E., gentile Christians greatly outnumbered Jewish Christians in the Roman Empire. These gentiles were increasingly separated from Jewish faith and culture.

Chapter Four

THE FAITH EXPANDS

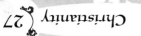

During the Roman persecution, the bishop of Antioch, Ignatius, was arrested and thrown to the lions in a Roman amphitheater.

Jesus' followers had spread beyond Palestine. Christians lived in communities in many parts of the empire. Some of their leaders worried that each Christian group might develop its own customs and stray from the movement's core beliefs. One of these leaders, Ignatius of Antioch, tried to unify all Christians. He urged each Christian community to admit only people who accepted that Jesus was God's son.

Ignatius also helped to create a ladder of authority in the emerging church. The leader of each local Christian group was called a bishop. That term came from the Greek word *episkopos*, meaning "overseer." A bishop oversaw the ceremonies involved in weekly worship. He also arranged for a place of worship. At first there were no formal churches, and worship took place in private homes. The bishop also kept in contact with bishops in neighboring towns. Assisting him in these duties were community elders called presbyters and deacons.

While the early church was unifying and organizing, it was also fighting for its life. Christians in some sectors of the empire were being persecuted. Non-Christian Romans sometimes assaulted

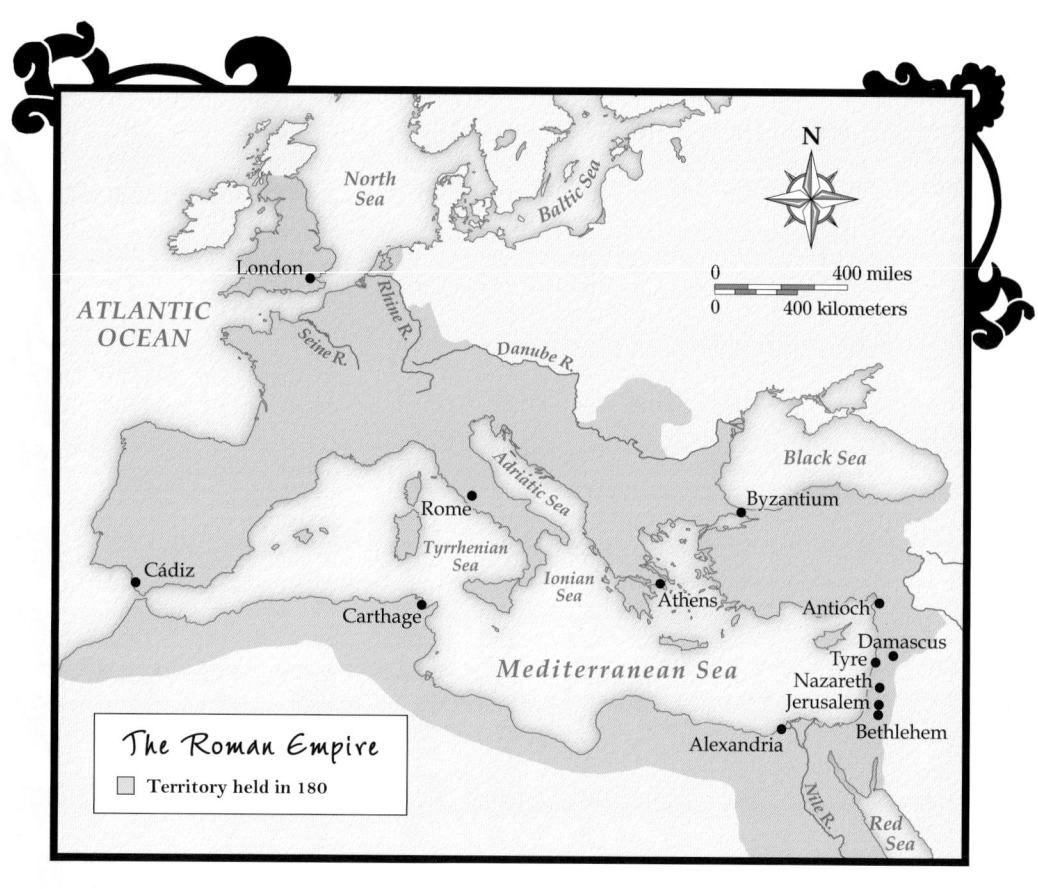

The Roman Empire

Territory held in 180

them. Some Christians were even arrested or killed by Roman authorities.

The Romans didn't persecute Christians because they worshipped a different god. The Romans acted because the Christians claimed that theirs was the only god. They refused to accept the existence of everyone else's gods, which made Christians widely unpopular. Another problem was that Christians refused to accept that the Roman emperors were semidivine. The government viewed this as a threat to its authority.

Christians sometimes were forced to face hungry animals in arenas in the Roman Empire.

As a result, anti-Christian persecutions occurred at times from the first to the third centuries. Most Christians responded with great courage, and the movement survived. The last and most destructive persecution took place in the early 300s.

During this period, Christianity received a big boost. Emperor Constantine I, who reigned from 306 to 337, befriended the Christians. He protected them and their worship. He also converted to the faith on his deathbed.

These events marked a major turning point for Christianity. All but one of the later Roman emperors were committed Christians. Under their rule, the church underwent rapid growth. In the late 300s, Christianity

A statue of Constantine in York, England, where he was proclaimed emperor in 306

A Christian Battle Emblem

One reason Constantine helped the Christians was an event that occurred in 312. In the midst of a civil war, Constantine led an army to Rome. He wanted to defeat his chief rival, Maxentius, who held the city. According to legend, Constantine told his men to paint the Christian symbol Chi-Rho on their shields. When the two armies fought at Rome's Milvian Bridge, Constantine was the winner. He credited much of his victory to the Christian God.

became Rome's official religion. With the church supported by the Roman imperial court and its great wealth, Christian worship became grander. The bishops took to wearing luxurious robes modeled after those of Roman noblemen.

Christian worship wasn't limited to wealthy circles, however. Devout Christians existed at all levels of society. This allowed the faith to survive even when the royal government disappeared. In the fifth and sixth centuries, the Roman Empire was overrun by tribal groups from central and northern Europe. This marked the start of what historians call the medieval era.

In early medieval times, Europe was made up of independent towns and small, unstable kingdoms. Amid the chaos, the popes and other church leaders provided some needed order. They maintained social and religious traditions from the past. In a way, the church guarded European civilization. Church leaders also sent priests to spread the Christian message to the many non-Christians who then lived across Europe. In time nearly all of them converted to the faith.

The church was less successful in Palestine. Because Christianity had been born there, Christians came to call this region the Holy Land. Many people journeyed there to visit the places where Jesus had preached. However, by the 600s, Palestine and other areas in what is now called the Middle East had come under the rule of Muslims, followers of the new faith of Islam. Christian leaders eventually sought to drive the Muslims out of the region and take control of the Holy Land. In 1095 Pope Urban II helped to organize the first of several large military expeditions. These became known as the Crusades. The crusaders had some success at first, but most of the expeditions ended in failure. Palestine

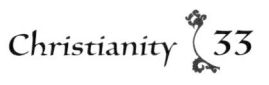

Thousands of soldiers waged war against the Muslims during the Crusades.

remained in Muslim hands.

About 200 years after the end of the Crusades, the church endured another major setback. This time it was rocked by a massive rebellion from within its own ranks. In 1517 a German monk named Martin Luther charged that the church had become corrupt. One

Martin Luther believed the path to salvation was through individual faith, not the church.

example of corruption involved Pope Leo X's plan to raise money to build St. Peter's Basilica. To raise funds, Leo sold indulgences—agreements to forgive people's sins regardless of whether they were sorry for what they had done. Luther and others demanded reforms in the church. When the pope refused, Luther was expelled from the Roman Catholic Church, and he established a new branch of Christianity, Lutheranism. In the years that followed, other Christian splinter groups formed. Because they all protested the traditional church, they became known collectively as Protestants.

The Catholic Church instituted reforms, which allowed it to survive. But it could not stop the great rebellion, which became known as the Reformation.

Main Branches of Christianity

The main Christian denominations and their major churches in the United States:

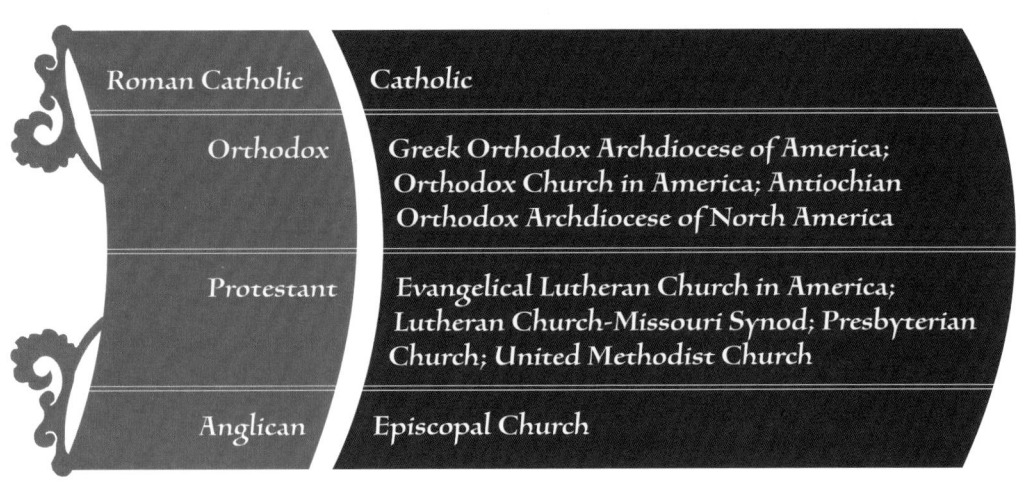

Roman Catholic	Catholic
Orthodox	Greek Orthodox Archdiocese of America; Orthodox Church in America; Antiochian Orthodox Archdiocese of North America
Protestant	Evangelical Lutheran Church in America; Lutheran Church-Missouri Synod; Presbyterian Church; United Methodist Church
Anglican	Episcopal Church

By the time Luther died in 1546, half of Europe had become Protestant. As time went on, many new Protestant denominations appeared. This not only made Christianity more diverse, but also ensured its continued success.

In England the breakaway church became the Church of England. The Anglicans kept most of the rituals and beliefs of the Roman Catholic Church but dropped their allegiance to the pope in Rome. Many religious scholars consider Anglican churches to be neither Protestant nor Catholic but a bridge that its followers hope will someday reunite the two groups.

Chapter Five

CHRISTIANS TODAY

Christianity has become the world's largest religion. About 39,000 Christian denominations exist. Their total membership is estimated to be more than 2 billion.

Of the three biggest Christian groups, the Roman Catholic Church is largest.

Numbering more than a billion worldwide, Catholics make up more than half of all Christians. Most of the rest of the Christians belong to various Protestant and Eastern Orthodox churches.

In addition to having many followers, these and other Christian groups are spread across most parts of the globe. From the 1400s to the 1800s, explorers and settlers from Spain, Portugal, France, England, and other Christian nations established colonies in North America, South America, Asia, the Pacific region, and elsewhere. They felt it was their duty to convert native peoples to the faith. Many natives were converted, and most of their descendants are devout Christians today. Some Christians, called missionaries, still travel far and wide to bring non-Christians into the faith.

Thus Christianity has become a prominent part of society and life in many parts of the world. It's not just that Christian beliefs and worship practices are widespread. Some Christian ideals and customs have become part of the social fabric of these countries. These customs include religious holidays, such as Easter and Christmas. In many places, even

A 125-foot (38-meter) statue of Jesus Christ, called Christ the Redeemer, *overlooks Rio de Janeiro, Brazil.*

Stores are often beautifully decorated for Christmas.

non-Christians celebrate Christmas. Shopping for Christmas gifts contributes much to the economies of the United States and other countries.

Similarly Christianity has greatly affected the arts. Museums across the globe are filled with paintings and sculptures depicting Jesus and other biblical figures. Musical pieces written to glorify God or to celebrate Jesus' life remain popular. For example, the majestic Handel's "Messiah" is widely performed every year. Films about Jesus and other biblical characters are made almost every year. One of the most popular in recent decades was Mel Gibson's *The Passion of the Christ*. It attracted huge audiences worldwide and earned more than $600 million.

There are few areas of life that Christianity has not

U.S. Catholic churches have no full-time priests. Almost 30 percent of shortage of priests and ministers. Perhaps the most important is a big pressing problems. However, modern Christianity faces some touched.

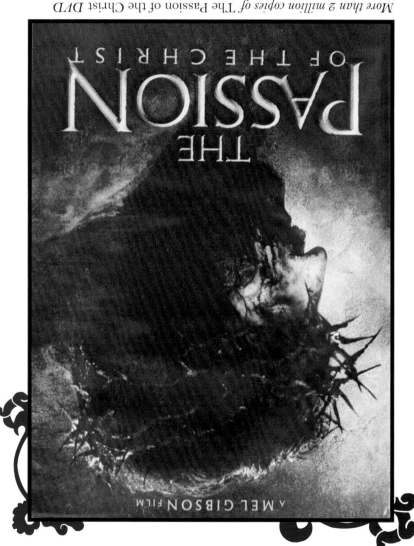

More than 2 million copies of The Passion of the Christ *DVD were sold on its first day of release.*

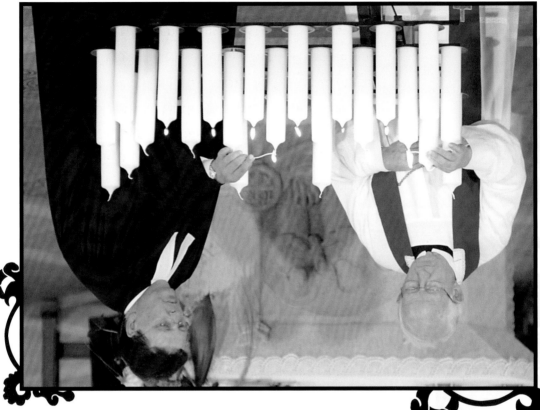

A Catholic priest (left) and a Protestant minister light candles during a combined service in Germany.

Since the 1970s, the number of young people entering the Catholic priesthood and Protestant ministries has greatly declined. In most Christian denominations, only 6 percent of the priests or ministers are under the age of 35. In comparison, 40 percent are older than 55. Studies have revealed many reasons for this shortage of clergy. One is that some members of the clergy, including Catholic priests, aren't allowed to marry.

They also must remain celibate, or refrain from sex. Many young people feel these are reasons enough not to pursue a career in the church. Another reason given is that churches, and religion in general, occupy a less central place in Western society today than they did in the past. So many young people see no strong reason to enter the clergy.

Still another factor is that many Christian groups don't allow women to become priests or ministers. Among them are Catholics, Eastern Orthodox, and Mormons. These and other churches that forbid female members of the clergy have a smaller segment of society to draw on for new leaders. By contrast most Anglican churches have female priests. Unitarian churches, most Methodist and Lutheran churches, and some Baptist churches also have female clergy. These churches therefore have an easier time finding recruits for the clergy.

Christianity has encountered problems of a different sort when some of its members have disagreed with scientific concepts. One of these is the scientific theory of evolution. It contends that humans and other mammals developed from simpler life forms over the ages. Some conservative groups and individuals have not accepted evolution. They argue that God created all life in a few days, as stated in the Bible.

 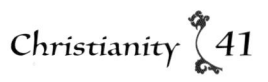

Another point of scientific disagreement among Christians is the age of Earth. Most Christians agree with scientists that the planet is more than 4 billion years old. Some conservative Christians disagree. They believe that Earth is only about 6,000 years old. This belief rests on selected passages in the Bible's first book, Genesis.

So modern Christians disagree about several issues.

Christians Against the Death Penalty

Some Christians oppose the death penalty and want to see it banned. They argue that this practice goes against God's will. In particular they point to the Ten Commandments. According to the Bible, these rules were handed down to the ancient Jews by God. One says: "Thou shall not kill." This commandment should apply to governments as well as to individuals, death penalty opponents argue. In their view, only God has the moral authority to take a life. So they believe executions are wrong.

The biblical story of creation has been the subject of many works of art.

But they all agree that 2,000 years ago God's son briefly appeared on Earth. The impact of that visit changed the world forever.

TIMELINE

4–6 B.C.E. Jesus Christ is born

Circa 30 C.E. Jesus is executed in Jerusalem

36 Saul of Tarsus, later called Paul, joins the early Christian movement

150 The Apostles' Creed, a statement of basic Christian beliefs, appears

306–337 Reign of the Roman emperor Constantine I, who befriends the Christians and converts to Christianity

400 The New Testament, as it is known today, is completed

1095 Pope Urban II calls for Christians to launch a holy crusade to free the Holy Land from Muslim control

1454 The Bible is the first book printed on a printing press

1517 German monk Martin Luther calls for reformation of the Catholic Church

1609 John Smyth establishes the Baptist Church, one of many Protestant denominations

1729 The Methodist Church, another prominent Protestant denomination, is founded by John Wesley

1948 The World Council of Churches—an organization that promotes unity and cooperation among all Christians—forms

2009 Hundreds of Christian leaders meet in Australia with leaders of other faiths to share ideas and promote world peace

Among the many world leaders who attended Pope John Paul II's funeral were three U.S. presidents. They were President George W. Bush and former presidents Bill Clinton and George H.W. Bush.

The first five books of the Old Testament are Genesis, Exodus, Leviticus, Numbers, and Deuteronomy. They are variously called the Five Books of Moses, the Pentateuch, and the Torah.

The Methodist Church was founded in 1787 in England by John Wesley. Under Wesley's guidance, the Methodist Church became involved in many social justice issues, including the abolition of slavery. Today more than 8 million people are members of the United Methodist Church.

The Presbyterian Church formed in 1560 in Europe. Among those responsible for founding the denomination were Ulrich Zwingli, John Calvin, Theodore Beza, and John Knox. Today about 2.5 million people belong to the Presbyterian Church in the United States.

Before the celebration of Easter is a 40-day period of fasting and repentance called Lent. The first day of Lent is called Ash Wednesday. During Ash Wednesday services, priests and ministers mark each person's forehead with a cross made from ashes. The placing of ashes on a person's forehead symbolizes mourning and penitence.

GLOSSARY

cardinals—leading bishops in the Catholic Church

clergy—group of people trained to conduct religious services and perform other duties

conservative—favoring tradition and opposing change

deacon—person who helps minister or preach

denomination—branch of a religion

divinity—being a God

evolution—scientific theory that higher life-forms developed from simpler ones over time

gentiles—people who are not Jewish

Messiah—superhuman figure whom the ancient Jews believed would come to rescue them from oppression

missionary—person who attempts to convert others to his or her faith

monastery—building or community in which devoutly religious people lead quiet, simple lives

monk—priest or other religious person who lives in a monastery

monotheism—belief in a single, all-powerful god

papal conclave—meeting in which cardinals choose a new pope

persecute—continually harass and hurt a person or group

repent—express regret for doing something wrong

resurrection—rising from the dead

revere—show great honor to

sacrament—sacred rite or ritual

salvation—God's forgiveness of someone's sins and acceptance of him or her into heaven

Holy Trinity—Christian concept according to which God has three distinct sides or personalities

FURTHER REFERENCE

Nonfiction

Bahr, Ann Marie B. *Christianity.* Philadelphia: Chelsea House Publishing, 2004.

Bowker, John Westerdale. *World Religions.* New York: DK Publishing, 2003.

Lace, William W. *Christianity.* San Diego: Lucent Books, 2005.

Fiction

Bradley, Kimberly Brubaker. *Leap of Faith.* New York: Dial Books for Young Readers, 2007.

Hershey, Mary. *10 Lucky Things That Have Happened to Me Since I Nearly Got Hit by Lightning.* New York: Wendy Lamb Books, 2008.

Woodson, Jacqueline. *Feathers.* New York: G.P. Putnam's Sons, 2007.

Internet Sites

FactHound offers a safe, fun way to find Internet sites related to this book. All of the sites on FactHound have been researched by our staff.

Here's all you do:

Visit *www.facthound.com*

FactHound will fetch the best sites for you!

INDEX

ABOUT THE AUTHOR

In addition to his acclaimed volumes on ancient civilizations, historian Don Nardo has written about the origins, history, beliefs, and historical and cultural impacts of several major religious groups and movements. Nardo lives with his wife, Christine, in Massachusetts.